Her House

And Other Poems

Donna Marie Merritt

Stairwell Books

Published by Stairwell Books
70 Barbara Drive
Norwalk
CT 06851 USA

A CIP catalogue record for this title is available from the British
Library

A CIP catalog record for this title is available from the Library of
Congress

ISBN: 978-1-939269-08-9

Printed and bound in the USA by ECPrinting.com

Layout design: Alan Gillott
Cover art: Wendell Minor

dedicated to Grandma Casteel...
I miss you and your way of looking at the world

Table of Contents

Washing Dishes 1

Bear Stick 3

PostScript 4

Sound of Insanity 5

my hand in yours 6

Then 7

Now 8

Applesauce! 9

Favorite 10

icicles 2011 11

In Sickness and in Health 12

Faith 13

Pretend 15

Spring Thaw 16

My Morning Walk 17

Darning Needles 19

rescued by a turtle 20

Psalm 46:10 21

An Afternoon with You 22

Wild Walks 23

Dancing Points 24

Thunder Tavern 25

Tiny Footprints 26

August 2, 2011 27

A Whale of a Haiku 28

Fish Food 29

Perfection Invention 30

Her House 31

College Call 32

Ideal Contestant 33

East Coast Weekend 34

Morris Spirit Shop 36

My Own Chelonian 37

Détente 38

Power Outage 39

Power Surge	40
Post-Storm Days	41
Heart(h)	42
a lesson in balance	43
I Live Within	44
Terrance in Disguise	45
In Support of President Barack Obama	46
For My Daughters	47
image	48
Call Me Grace	49
Host	50
Saint Patrick's Day	51
almost	52
Staying In	53
Our Chair	54
Teaching to the Test	55
Are We There Yet?	56
Peaches	57
Dawn Drive	59
Dancing with You	60
Dust	61

Washing Dishes

Hands glide, slide,
slip through sudsy
water, warm, soft,
inviting me back
I stand
on a chair
beside Grandma
at the kitchen sink
Backyard sun peeks
through space
between curtains,
touches her face
She shows me how
to plug the drain,
add a few drops
of soap, let the
running water
create bubbles
that rise to the top
...*pop!* or float away
like the dandelion seeds
we blow together

I think it's magic
think it's a game
we are playing
just us two
Grandma never makes
work feel like work
and always makes
me feel like there is
nowhere she'd rather be
than with me
no matter what
we are doing
I stand at the sink
on the brink
of tears,

thankful
for traveling forty-
something years
to this memory,
thankful
for a dishwasher
on the fritz ⁄⁄

Bear Stick

I carry
a bear stick
when I walk
in woods,
an autumn
wanderer.
I am aware
it won't scare
the bear
but
I report
it makes me
feel safer,
magic wand
of sorts.
Poof!
Take that,
bear.
I dare
you. //

PostScript

Plain planks
sank beneath
my shoes
avoiding spots
to fall through
i came across
to talk to
a still creature
bonus feature
of the marsh
i had thought
to converse
but blue heron
did not stay
seemed terse
as if i were an
intrusion! and
in confusion
flew away
no interview
such thankS ⁄⁄

Sound of Insanity

She
opens her
mouth
It seems
she screams
with enough
might to
make the
earth shake
No one
comes
running
She is left
with only
vibration
humming
in her throat ⫽

my hand in yours

lying in bed
nothing said
gentle squeeze
is all I need
side by side
fingers entwined
sleepy team
drifts to dreams ⫰

Then

While the house snoozed
the fog slithered in, oozed,
moved over it, through it,
reared back, swallowed it...
a snake devouring its prey ⫽

Now

Piano, bought used,
could stand a tuning
we can not afford
Shelves rest nearby
rescued from oblivion
when they closed your office
Is this what poor feels like?
Now
>One child plays
>Clair de Lune
>One child fills shelves
>With her art

No,
This is what rich feels like ⫽

Applesauce!

Worked
for weeks
Changing
Revising
Arranging
Analyzing
Fed it to
shredder
in the end
After all
I had already
mutilated
the words
Three days
later in the
shower
head back
eyes closed
warm river
caressing
my body
rivets running
over me
the poem
came to me
in its entirety
in a completely
different form
than the one
I had tried to
force upon it ⫻

Favorite

My favorite
thing on a
winter night,
New England...
Sink into
oversized chair
Stare
at flickering
flames you have
coaxed into being
Sip our cabernet
Warm our souls
Lean against you
as you match wits
with the crossword
Pick up paper,
pencil, Coax a
verse into being
too
so it can share
this perfect
moment
with us ⁄⁄

icicles 2011

skies cry, tears fly, freeze
on shutters; frostbitten house
shudders, begs spring's warmth ⫽

In Sickness and in Health

Chin drops
Dribble of drool pools
in lips' cracked corner
No one warns her
of the changing
of the guard
But she feels it
Head snaps up
Jared!
Feels it in the
way the chair
moves, in the
way the wheels
groove, and
Jared!
—*Right behind you*—
    Momentarily shocked
    delightedly reassured
    A person re-emerges
    Peek-a-boo!

Jared's handkerchief
deftly catches the
gurgle set free
with her giggle
before her eyes
lose recognition
and
chin drops ⫽

Faith

In the midst of
morning madness
the doorbell rings
Are you confused
in today's world?
—May I help you?—
We've been talking
to your neighbors
—May I help you?—
Friend, we can show you
The One True Way
—No thank you—
I close the door,
annoyed

I am frustrated
with myself for
behaving rudely
What I meant to
say, calmly, is that
Faith is a personal thing
"As for me and my house
we will serve the Lord"
The Lord said nothing
about going door to door
about imposing beliefs
about smug pity in your eyes
because I would not let you save me

I believe
in a loving God
who cares not how you label yourself
but welcomes everyone,
sinner, believer,
anyone who tries to do right in this world...
kind people who give their lives to others...
I do not think He will close heaven's gates
against anyone who loves
because love
is of God

That is what I meant
to say, calmly, rather
than close the door
as you walk away
shaking your heads
leaving the damned behind ⫻

Pretend

Just pretend
Just pretend you are okay
each day
Do not let anyone know
you are slow
ly going out
of your mind
one bite at a time

Talk
Walk
Laugh smile
One step of the mile

Just pretend
Just pretend each day
you are okay
Do not let anyone slow
ly know you are
coming out
of your bind
one mite at a time //

Spring Thaw

Days longer
Mind stronger
Heart lighter
Smile brighter

Hope...around corner
Soul...growing warmer ⁄⁄

My Morning Walk

was
> vermicular concrete
> writhing with life
perpendicular displays
of velvet green, not
a blade out of place
in suburbialand
> pile of cedar mulch
> ready for spreading
> smelled before seen
school children waiting
for bus, hoping it might
pass them just this once
summer tugging like
sound of "Supper!"
soaring through a
1950s neighborhood
> ivy resting, nestling
> among crevices
> in stone walls built
> when Connecticut
> hills were cleared
flowers sprouting, shouting colors
bursting forth from earth's dirt seams
> birds serenading as if I were
> the animated Snow White
pinecone graveyard
no grieving visitors
> beer can in bush
> hallowed teen ground
open horse pasture
inviting lazy days
> mailbox decapitated
> by long-gone snowplow
> unmended, left to fend
> for itself
wildflowers lingering
mingling with litter
alongside road

passing under boasting boughs
crunching last year's foliage
under foot
broken branches
survivors of winter snow
but unprepared
for gentle wearing
of spring storms
and
sweet softness
of brooks and streams
meandering in, around
Watertown
was
my morning walk ⚘

Darning Needles

dragonflies shimmer
in bright sunlight, scatter all
in pond-frenzied flight ⁄⁄

rescued by a turtle

the heat of the walk
was crushing till sight of a
turtle refreshed me

shedding sun-soaked log
abandoning perch sliding
into the coolness

for a brief moment
i was that turtle gliding
past cares in the now ⁄⁄

Psalm 46:10

In...out...
Breathe.
No need

to shout.

Center.
Be still.
I will

enter

your heart.
Be
with me.

Soul art. ⫽

An Afternoon with You

Sandy shore
Beach bar
Young crowd
Live band
Sign saying "We
card *everyone.*
No exceptions"
(They wave us in)
We order
afternoon drinks
on this lazy
summer day
And then when
time to pay
discover
that neither of us
has brought a wallet
I search my beach bag
You search your pockets
We put what money we find
on the table like
a couple of college kids
Hey! Just enough
for one more drink
with two straws

I would not trade this bliss
for cocktails at the Ritz ⁄⁄

Wild Walks

Squirrels, birds,
chipmunks
meeting
under a tree
enjoying a
bountiful breakfast
and
in that same yard
three bunnies sitting
as still and alert as
chocolate counterparts
on a store shelf
Two holding position
One getting nervous
hopping into the street
a car missing it by
a hare

Dear deer curious
about me, not curious
enough to stick around

Gaggle of geese
parading as one
arrogantly claiming
the town ball field

Two skittish turkeys
scooting off the path
disappearing into safety

And
one hundred fifty
determined
turtles taking a
gamble, ambling
across JFK
causing delay
as flights slow
to turtle time //

Dancing Points

Sunken Garden Poetry Festival
ends with a sunken sun

As we leave
a self-contained field of fireflies
greets us
dancing among the grass
as we pass
bouncing beams
here! burst! there!
guiding us, pointing home
We find our way
The fireflies stay to meet
other dazed wanderers

They are the unspoken poems—
these tiny points of light ⁄⁄

Thunder Tavern

Strolling
Cape Cod streets
the skies open
We duck into a tavern
Eye the one empty table
in the middle of the fray
Glance out the door
at the downpour
Decide to stay
Your meal arrives
before your appetizer
It comes when it comes
the waitress says
There is hot sauce on my
sandwich, not the mayo
I requested
*Sometimes they make
substitutions
Sometimes they don't*
But the cabernet is good
and they have Berkshire
beer for you
Soon we are not only
dry and warm
but toasty
Can't you see?
Singing along with
the Marshall Tucker Band
Free fallin' with Tom Petty
Thankful
for sudden storms ⁄⁄

Tiny Footprints

And what do you find
Sandpiper, sandpiper?

Scuttle, scurry, fly
turn by and by
back again to sand
From sea toward land

Sandpiper, sandpiper
Are you on rewind? ⁄⁄

August 2, 2011

I was not
prepared
for these
majestic creatures
alongside our boat
Groups of two, three, four, five
Mother nursing calf
    Teenager stopping mid-text
      to watch
    Whining child
      suddenly mesmerized
Humpbacks
spouting, spraying
displaying tremendous
tails, sailing
thriving, diving
breaching, teaching
power, grace
beyond the space
of our secure
insecurities ⌀

A Whale of a Haiku

phytoplankton, green
on white that highlight giants
of fluorescent sea ⁄⁄

Fish Food

They were shouting
from shore pointing
waving us in
It was then that
we noticed we were
the only ones left
in what had been
an ocean of people
Momentarily stunned by
the dorsal fin twenty
feet behind us I
did not move as
quickly as you and
struggled against the
water and the panic
for sixty seconds or so
before you saw I was
not with you and
came back for me
It was only a sunfish
(one or two THOU
sand pounds of it)
but no one knew
that then and my
heart may beat
this fast
forever //

Perfection Invention

I wade out alone
unroll the straw mat
adjust the bathing suit
around my middle-aged fat
Lean back
Sun on face
Ocean in ears
Close my eyes
and I am twenty
a bikini revealing
my perfect body
On shore they squint
Shade their eyes
Try to get a better look
at this young woman
on the sandbar
oblivious to her
flawless beauty ⁄⁄

Her House

Home.
The dunes were
eroding more seriously.
One day the shore
would be no more.
Neighbors abandoned, sold
abodes. A few brave ones—
brave, rich ones—moved
their dwellings to safer
ground. She looked around,
found she was the
only denizen for miles
along that coast. She
made toast and tea
waited patiently
watched the sea
through her curtainless
window. This widow
was content to see
water's edge move ever
closer. One day welcome
waves slapped at front
steps. She smiled in sweet
anticipation. Years ago she
had decided her house
would be the vessel to
carry her to her husband.
Home. ⫽

College Call

It breaks my heart
to hear you cry
I want to drive
through the states
straight
to your dorm
scoop you up
and hold you
like when you were little
had scraped a knee
or someone had hurt
your feelings
I want to make it better

Instead
I tell you that
you will settle in
it will get easier
you will do great

I hang up
unsure if I was
reassuring you
or me
then sob
silently ⁄⁄

Ideal Contestant

Do you ever watch
those game shows
where a player talks
of peaches-and-cream life
wonderful spouse, adorable kids
Just once wouldn't you like to hear
"My spouse is a lying, lazy, loud jerk
and my kids are rotten to the core
and I am on this show to win tons
of money so I can leave them all!"
No?
Oh, I thought it would be hilarious ⁄⁄

East Coast Weekend

Friday
sunshine
eighty degrees
We prepare

Saturday
cloud-covered sunrise
air perfectly still

Mid-morning
          patio
chairs in—check
umbrella down—check
table flipped—check
          bottled
water—check
milk—check
wine—double check
          packaged
ice—check
batteries—sold out
chocolate—check

Saturday afternoon
a downpour
fifteen minutes
then a break
then rain again
on and off till
downpours, breaks
converge; water whispers
she's on her way

Late afternoon
Eat a little
chocolate

Evening
Drink a bit of
wine

Saturday night
Go to sleep
and wait

Sunday
four a.m.
Wake to winds
with frighten-
ing intensity

Mid-morning
Sheets of rain so thick
we can't see past
the window
Up and down
cellar steps
every half hour with
mops, towels, buckets
but we are thankful
for power, pray
for the half million
without

Sunday afternoon
Rain ends
Doors, windows
open
Cellar drying
Skies brightening

Monday morn
brilliant dawn ⚟

Morris Spirit Shop

Men on front porch
lean back in chairs, looking out from under
New England caps, permanent extensions of personalities
hound at their feet, arching one eyebrow noncommittally
at passersby

Evening air brings with it a nip
Dog days of summer will soon take leave
leaving us to wonder what we did wrong,
why they packed their bags long before they had worn out
their welcome ⁄⁄

My Own Chelonian

chelonian, a
lone again? you are too slow
to race status quo ⫽

Détente

Red-shouldered hawk
extends strong wings
over three feet as
it circles midair

American crow
extends black wings
almost three feet as
it dives at hawk

Hawk and crow
Crow and hawk
Flash of night
Splash of earth

Crow claw, hawk beak
caw, screech, bird speak
Dart out, swoop in
Who will win?

I stand in awe of
this amazing display
this aerial attack
Corvus versus *Buteo*

But when

Great   Horned   Owl
invades their space
crow and hawk chase
the outsider away

together

Momentary peace
in the sky till a cry
shatters it—they are at it
again ⫽

Power Outage
(CT, October 2011)

So
this is what it's like
No humming of anything
electronic
Only the crack and cackle
of the fire—
the only sound
the only light
the only warmth ⁄⁄

Power Surge

glass of red wine, words
by candlelight, power out
forces power in ⁄⁄

Post-Storm Days

First rays
display exhales
frozen in midair
I burrow in deeper
Stew gets up to start the fire
puts water on the grill for coffee—him
      tea—me
The days are sunny enough
to warm the house a bit
but still we wear layers
While there is light
I read and crochet
He reads, does crosswords
A cooler sits in snow
filled with snow and a
few salvaged things from the fridge
that we pick through for lunch
At night we grill potatoes
      eat by candlelight
        play Scrabble
We crawl between cold sheets
fully clothed, snuggle in
pull quilts and covers to chin
pray to wake to power

But we will miss this ⫽

Heart(h)

flickering fingers
of flame bursting into life
dying to give warmth ⫽

a lesson in balance

Usually
he watches tv
she gets on the computer
they learn new things, minds make connections

Yet
this week
no tv
no internet
they have learned from one another
they have connected in a new way
    Now
    holding hands, they sit close
    staring at the fire they built together
    secretly praying not to forget ⁄⁄

I Live Within

I need quiet space
where fear can be quelled

Time to pull into myself
    turtle in shell
Place to contemplate
    hermit in cave
Room to change
    bug in cocoon
Safety of love
    child in warm womb

I need quiet space to
Breathe. Begin again. ⁄⁄

Terrance in Disguise

skeleton hidden
clothed in coat of glowing white
fooling even me

you wear winter well
puffy white sleeves on thin limbs
death does not find you ⫽

In Support of President Barack Obama
(February 2012)

May I suggest that mudslingers
    clean the dirt
    from under clawing nails
    scrub expressions
    raw of smirking filth
    wash treasonous mouths
    with disinfecting soap

Let's have a poetry party in the White House ⫽

For My Daughters

I have loved you since before you were born
Unconditionally
There is not one thing you could do or say
to make me walk away
You are my rays of sun
      petals opening to dawn's light
      stars shooting across sky
      dolphins dancing through waves
          Pure Joy
When I look at you
I see, all at once,
babies sleeping in my arms as I breathe in sweet newborn skin,
toddlers needing only a tiny tickle or funny face to fall into
hysterical giggles, scraped-knee preschoolers seeking a bandage
and a kiss, adoring school kids who are sure I know everything,
eye-rolling teens who think I know nothing, young adults who
admit I might know a *little*

You are my heart, my essence
My daughters, you are my *all*
Despite my bumbles as I learn to be a parent (still), know
always, always
I love you. I am proud of you.
Saying,
"These are my *daughters"* brings indelible delight to my soul ⁄⁄

image

if only there were
no mirrors we would be young
for eternity ⫽

Call Me Grace

When did my world change
from french fries and milkshakes
to high fiber and portion control?
When did I exchange
spiked heels and flattering fashion
for flats and clothes that hide me?
How did someone attach these
under-eye bags and sun spots
to my face without my knowing?
Why did I shrink half an inch?
Why are there handles to pinch?
Why can't it be a cinch
to grow older?

I am trying to do so with grace
Why the f— ain't it workin' that way? //

Host

You
swing open the door
welcome me warmly
hang my coat
bring a bouquet
Such a display
of hospitality
Spring, you are
one fine host ⁄⁄

Saint Patrick's Day

For some
St. Patrick's Day is
green beer
For some
corned beef and cabbage
For some
parades
For some
wearin' o' the green
And some
Irish songs and stories
For me
it's the day of your stem cell transplant
Eight months of aggressive chemo, hospital stays,
     setbacks and scares
          led us to that day
For me
St. Patrick's Day is
your recovery
Three years, cancer-free
That is worth
good food and drink, processions and pageantry,
     drums and pipes
          and snake-driving saints
It's all for you, baby—
this celebration of Life—
It's all for you ⌀

almost

slice the wrap
unwind it
tug it off
slowly
insert screw
turn turn turn
clockwise
rise rise rise
pop
air
take cork
turn turn turn
counterclockwise
release
from screw
set aside
pour bottle
glug
glug
look at it
hold it to the light
sweet red liquid
after this ritual
it is almost a shame
to drink it
almost ⁄⁄

Staying In

Red heels
drop to floor
as you explore
lips, neck
Fingers rest
on breast
—it's yours
Nipple stiffens
Squeeze it
into your mouth
Tongue tastes
delicious flesh
Suck—
pull mound in,
push mound out
Fingers move
down,
find wetness
between legs...
Let's store
this bliss under
"how to spend
Saturday night" ⫽

Our Chair

The kids think
we are ridiculous
not letting them sit
in "our" chair
This is a second marriage
for both of us
My furniture is from
my first marriage
Stew added things
from his but
nothing belonged to
us
We shopped every weekend
for a month
sitting on chair after chair
in store after store
until we sat on "our" chair and a half
with room for both butts
where we were
a young couple crazy in love
a comfy old married pair
at once
It's the one thing in the house
that belongs only to
us
So the kids will
just have to adjust ⁄⁄

Teaching to the Test

We train kids
     to take tests
like training rats
     to run a maze
We take the joy
     out of discovery
We make them memorize
     instead of problem-solve
We ask that they work alone
     instead of in groups
We require them to interact
     with a piece of paper
rather than communicate
     with each other
We forget our real goal—
     to inspire life-long learning
Life-long test-takers stop
     at the end of a test,
     the dead-end of a maze
Life-long learners
     scale the walls of ignorance,
     explore the world ⁄⁄

Are We There Yet?

When is mid-life?
That depends on date of death
We can not really know
Oh, maybe as we are dying
we will take our last moments
of clear thought to calculate it
But I think it will not matter much
We will be considering things
of more importance
like whether our presence here mattered
whether we touched a life or two
did something good
offered kindness
honored and loved our families
  as deeply as they deserved

Still, I wonder, at this precise hour,
Is my time exactly half over?
Do I have years yet?
Was mid-mark decades ago?
Never mind—makes my head spin
to contemplate whether
  there is an open track before me
    I have taken half my laps
      or am crossing the finish line
This is my race, my pace
I will focus on today
I will walk, not run
I will stop when I need a breath
I will not turn to see if death
  is gaining ⁄⁄

Peaches

She could fit in the palm of your hand
when she was born. She was cute.
Still, I told her right from the start,
I don't like dogs.
I had given in for the sake
of my daughters.
When she was old enough, at eight weeks,
to be separated from her mother,
we brought this bundle of fur home.
I held her on my lap in the car,
but only because she was scared.
After all, she had just left her
mother and siblings. Yet, I told her,
I don't like dogs.
When I lifted her from the kitchen and set her down
one step into the family room (she was afraid
to make the leap), I told her,
I don't like dogs.
When we replaced the carpet in the family room
because training had not gone well at first,
you know what I told her
(though I did like the new carpet).
When she barked incessantly
every time someone entered,
When she ran in circles
waiting to go outside,
When she shook with excitement
eager for a treat,
When my back ached from shoveling a path
and clearing an area in the snow-covered yard
so she could do her business, I told her sternly,
I don't like dogs.
When she forgot she was playing fetch
and wandered away to lie in the sun or
When she curled up on my lap,
I told her, as I petted her,
I don't like dogs.
When I carried her from the kitchen and set her down
on the chair because she was too weak and sick

to do it on her own,
I looked in her eyes and remembered how she danced
around for twelve years as if I were praising her
each time I told her
I don't like dogs.
When I cleaned up her vomit and feces,
When I cooked bacon and eggs and steak
and tried to coax her to eat,
When I carried her outside to feel the cool grass
one more time, I told her,
I don't like dogs
and she seemed comforted.
When her eyes glazed over,
When my daughters and I held her
for the last time, I told her,
You're a good dog.
I will miss you...
I think she knew. ⟋⟍

Dawn Drive

Connecticut hills,
morning mist rises, water
glistens at day's glow //

Dancing with You

is wonderful
But sometimes
late at night
if I am alone
at home I
turn on the radio
Dance by myself
Move in ways I
would never move
in public
Hips pulsate
Body lowers to floor
Rises once more
Head tilts back
Eyes close
Hands slide over
ass, Shoulders
go left, right
Snap, clap
Twist, spin
Step, kick
Feel sexy for a song
Laugh at how I
would appear
to anyone watching
Then think
Who gives a shit?
Take another
rhythmic roll,
another erotic
stroll through
the family room ⌇

Dust

The first question I will ask
God at the end of my life
will not be a religious or
philosophical one, but a
practical question rooted in
curiosity. *What is the purpose
of dust?* You clear the dust
and it returns. Again. Again.
If God keeps putting it in
front of us, over and over,
in plain sight, maybe we
are missing something. Is
it an all-answer energy
source? Can it be converted
into food to eliminate world
hunger? Does it possess
medicinal value that can
cure cancer? And if I can not
figure out why dust matters,
how can I be sure I know
what anything means—life,
death, the reasons we exist?
Look at a sunbeam aimed
right at your table, radiance
sent millions of miles to high-
light the minute particles falling
silently around us with no
clue what they are communicating!
Or will God shrug His holy shoulders,
laugh a belly laugh that
echoes through every valley
and say, *It's just dust. Do not
take everything so seriously. //*

Donna Marie Merritt

Poet, Writer, Columnist, Editor, Educator! Donna Marie Merritt is all these and more. In her long career, she has contributed stories and poems to school reading programs, written articles and columns on education and parenting, has worked as a curriculum editor, and has written over three dozen teachers' guides—all during or after her years as a teacher (from kindergarten to classes for adults).

Donna Marie is also the author of 15 award-winning math and science books for children with over 130,000 copies sold to date.

However, it is as a poet that Donna Marie Merritt shines as a mother, wife, and soul searcher. She has been able to transcend a period of personal heartache to write the "Poetry for Tough Times" series: *What's Wrong with Ordinary? Poems to Celebrate Life* (2012); *Cancer, A Caregiver's View* (2011); and *Job Loss, A Journey in Poetry* (2010), all from Avalon Press. Her poems have appeared in magazines such as *Highlights High Five* and American Library Association's *Book Links*. Her work has also been included in several anthologies: *Caduceus*, volumes 9 and 10, by the Yale Medical Group (2012, 2013); *Olives, Now and Then: poems in honor of Donald Hall* by the Connecticut Poetry Society (2011); and *Dear One: A Tribute to Lee Bennett Hopkins* by the National Council of Teachers of English (2009).

Visit her at www.DonnaMarieBooks.com or learn more at http://en.wikipedia.org/wiki/Donna_Marie_Merritt.

Other publications available from Stairwell Books

First Tuesday in Wilton	Ed. Rose Drew and Alan Gillott
The Exhibitionists	Ed. Rose Drew and Alan Gillott
The Green Man Awakes	Ed. Rose Drew
Carol's Christmas	N.E. David
Fosdyke and Me and Other Poems	John Gilham
frisson	Ed. Alan Gillott
Feria	N.E. David
Along the Iron Veins	Ed. Alan Gillott and Rose Drew
A Day at the Races	N.E. David
Gringo on the Chickenbus	Tim Ellis
Running With Butterflies	John Walford
Foul Play	P. J. Quinn
Late Flowering	Michael Hildred
Scenes from the Seedy Underbelly of Suburbia	Jackie Simmons
Pressed by Unseen Feet	Ed. Rose Drew and Alan Gillott
York in Poetry Artwork and Photographs	Ed. John Coopey and Sally Guthrie
Poison Pen	P.J.Quinn
Rosie and John's Magical Adventure	The Children of Ryedale District Primary Schools

For further information please contact rose@stairwellbooks.com

www.stairwellbooks.co.uk